CLUTTER JAR

Christopher Horton was born in Camden, grew up in Oxfordshire and now lives in rural Kent with his wife and two young children. After a period of time teaching English as a second language in China, he went on to live in London for sixteen years where he worked in a number of roles including as a housing officer and town planner. He is a devotee of experimental electronic music.

Also by Christopher Horton

Perfect Timing   (tall-lighthouse press, 2021)

CONTENTS

For Carol

ISBN: 978-1-917617-44-4

Cover designed by Aaron Kent

Edited and Typeset by Aaron Kent

Broken Sleep Books Ltd
PO BOX 102
Llandysul
SA44 9BG

Clutter Jar

Christopher Horton

Broken Sleep Books

BEFORE THE CLINKING OF GLASSES

To us – the first to eclipse
the moon, to re-arrange the stars,
to peer into the open mouths

of baited copperheads, to howl across
the frozen tundra with packs
of hungry arctic wolves, to sip

sweet nectar from Hebe's golden cup.
Forget the try-hards, the fakes,
the closeted fools of modern youth,

who would sooner have their brains frozen,
their tissue cryogenically revived,
than learn the ways of jellyfish.

Recall the promises we made,
the songs we sang to keep us warm
on the most unforgiving nights.

How we thought ourselves immortal,
that we could transform base metals
into gold and split the subatomic

particles left in light and air
with nothing more than words,
as if our lives depended on it.

EXPERTS

We like to forget that in fact everything in our life is chance.

— Sigmund Freud

There are those who calculate
the prospective density of snow,
the day it will come, where it will fall,
how many people will, in all probability,
stay off work because of it…

…and there are those who walk gingerly
on the thick ice – with measuring devices
and high-vis jackets – to gauge
when the covered roads will reveal
old markings through sludge and grit…

…and there are lives given over
to predicting the median velocity of wind
in Iowa years from now,
and others dedicated to forecasting
the quantity of frogs and fish that will drop
from a specific league of sky.

But you and I have slipped the radar,
bucked the trend, as we head out
where traffic darts from every angle
and, further on, the Thames does what it wants,
laving and lapping against the quays.

Night might steal us away
under its star-spun cloak.
Even this is measured by astronomers.

Best put a hand on your heart
and feel how sometimes, just sometimes,
it jumps or skips a beat.

THE OLD CROWD

And when you left that chilly room,
where real life seemed plenty real enough,
did the old crowd secretly reassemble
around the glow of a space heater
to go through a set of scripted scenarios,
each one pre-empting your next retorts?

Or, as part of a rehearsed improv approach –
necessarily structured but not overly –
did words simply bubble to the surface
as if gifted from a celestial source
to be recalled, condensed, and then repeated
for the live performance?

The acting was sufficiently heartfelt
for you to think life possessed spontaneity,
albeit you always had an inkling
their slightly exaggerated mannerisms
were not entirely *felt* or from a place
that could be called *deep*, even *authentic*.

What would happen if you walked in
unannounced and caught a snippet
of tomorrow's scenes being played out?
Suppose, there in the round, you witness
the silences, the gaps between two voices,
then hear a slow and persistent breathing,
where your own lines are meant to be.

SHAOSHAN

We went there because it was where Mao was born.
The son of a disciplinarian, forced into an unhappy marriage
at thirteen, I only later read he tried to run away.
Was he happy when growing up? I asked at the time.
Of course, you said, but something made you speak quietly,
each word was swallowed back inside your throat.

The picture I took shows you immaculately dressed.
Your one brown suit was always unmarked. I came to learn
it matched every season and amounted to a week's wages.
The look on your face is familiar but still hard to read.
It conceals that other you, the non-tour guide version.
We only ever had the one discussion about Tiananmen.

When you finally told me about your younger brother,
it was two months from this hot day in Shaoshan.
Difficult to comprehend the fear that would make a man
jump from the open window of a provincial lecture room
when they came for him with batons in the reckoning.

This was not the place to have that discussion,
not in Mao's own village where ladies danced
and sang to venerate *The Glorious Revolution*,
whilst twirling red ribbons in time and where,
as my questions fell, you lost your voice.

POSTHUMOUS

Shame on the hive's ungrateful bees
as they compete without pause or reflection
on the sublime nature of unconditional love.
On hearing the news, their keeper has passed away,
they carry-on as before, unmoved.
At times like this, you could hate their cold
buzz conferring on a single cause.

Each time their keeper held aloft the brood frame
a stretching light shone through his protector,
caught his eyes, transmuting them amber.
The same way a narrow beam
enters a chapel's apse, changing
the molecules of all it falls upon.

It was the bees he lived for. They defined him.
He would study their technique and poise
and, through this, a strong admiration formed.
The bees would not think to reciprocate.
Only pleasing the queen bee matters for them.
Besides, he largely evaded their ultraviolent range.

See the giant mind of the superstructure,
the nectar chutes shot from their rucksacks.
Witness the teeming swarm of the minions
as they form and reform, meticulously
revising what went before. Until the last drop
of all they have to give, is completely spent
with no room whatsoever for sentiment.

SOMETHING NOT QUITE PLACED

Why quibble over the genetic disposition
that shaped, so completely, my third nipple?

I would blow your belly button
as others blow out eggs, should you allow it;

would massage the pads beneath your toes,
were this accepted currency. Don't laugh

when I tell you how you once startled me,
your eyes, a poor comparison to rare gems

or, worse still, opals, but fashioned
out of something not quite placed

as if you were an alien. Let's say,
for the sake of posterity, you are an alien.

Would you kindly lose me in your flesh,
then convert me by hypnosis, to the merits

of metamorphosis? Suppose I lip-sync
the words that first fall from your mouth,

so that all distinctions in our language
become a mere irrelevance

and sound trips unchallenged
in the precise scattering of waves.

PLASTIC SEAHORSES

What you think of now is an ad hoc army
of small plastic seahorses afloat amidst
a wide-spectrum of colours, bobbing across
a vast ocean, filling that ocean as far
as your mind's eye takes you. The seahorses
are spilled from a container-boat upturned.

The crew might be rescued but nothing can be done
for their load. Held in a single palm,
each one taken by itself could be a curio,
or at least prized and wanted in that moment.

A world could be imagined from just one seahorse.
It could have a name, a life of its own.
Here, in the sea, the ownerless beasts
are potent, a threat. Here, they imitate

the sea-life beneath, and are at odds with it.
Washed ashore, a few might be given a proper home
or, just as feasibly, be swallowed by a giant turtle
to lodge, misaligned, in its guts, cutting short its story

as it heads out with its loyal bale but now too injured
to keep up. Others might be picked for refuse,
buried, or burned, still to be resurrected,
still to hold out their stubborn moulded form
for a thousand years, ownerless, unclaimed.

TWO MEN FIGHTING

South London, outside the Little Crown,
early summer evening, two men, tanked up,
throwing punches towards each other,
at first, on the pavement then in the road.

When I say *men*, these were old men, worn out,
beaten-down; men who should know better.
No one could keep them apart as they fought
and anyway it seemed like a regular thing.

Sure, some tried to break it up but they kept on,
occasionally making contact, more often hitting
the thick stem of air that stood between them.
The landlord leant on the doorway, yawning,

If it was a spectacle, they hardly saw each other
and the target was everywhere about them.
When they finally rested, they held each other
for breath, stumbling into each other's range.

A hot sticky street aroma came upon us all,
until no one really watched for an end anymore.
It wasn't boredom that stopped the onlooking,
more an appreciation they needed space.

In truth, they could not have been more unified
as they were there in the street, alone together,
punching out all that had fled into them,
taking on every year lost.

ON ACCOUNT OF HIS RECURRING DREAM

It began with him digging, spade in both hands,
head down, arms piston-regular, focused.
Why he was doing this and who would cover over
the hole, was never fully questioned.

An internal logic was at work that made this normal.
There was no reason to feel he hadn't known
this was the right time to be digging
or that he hadn't made the most of things.

The location was familiar. He didn't know
how he had arrived at this place but he had a hunch
he could find it on a map. There were signifiers.
It was a place where thistles and hemlock grew.

When the ground was opened-up to the size of a calf,
he put down his spade and lay face up in the hole.
Briefly, the sky became his only view.

In the half-light, earth filled the gap between
his sides, the space above. He tightened himself,
each muscle, taking the extra weight upon his chest,

his arms, his legs, his face, until there was nothing,
just darkness, and the last inhale of stale air
held deep inside his throat was all he had to keep.

AMBITION

When the subject comes up, our voices lower, our faces change.
It's ugly, I mean *ambition,* we are told, is ugly.
We have those things we share as secrets and they don't feel wrong,
even if we wouldn't bring them to our work places
or release them to our friends without prior agreement.
Instead, we confer in hushed tones on long canal walks.
We collaborate whilst in the aisles of the local DIY store.
We keep lists and little notes that we drop between the skirting boards.
You tell me one day that we are behind schedule,
that I'm full of hot air. On reflection, I confess you have a point.

When you went out, I pulled back those skirting boards
to find things were different from how I remembered them.
Your notes consisted of a crystal-clear logic. To my surprise,
this was where you also kept a vintage wall-clock ticking
precisely next to a list of baby names and a picture of us at our best.
My notes and scribbles reminded me of the man who woke early
in a south-facing room and witnessed what he thought was the sun
rising above the horizon like a new crown, like the perfect sign,
only to then see it rising all over again.

FLAT ON THE HIGH STREET

Now do nothing except rejoice in the coming together
of duvet and skin. When you finally bother to stretch,
your metabolic rate will be measured by the short-lived
dripping of the shower head, your eyelids still sealed
and symmetrically adorned with diamonds of sleep.

When a phone buzzes, give it the silent treatment.
When the washing up, without warning, subsides further
into the unplumbed depths of the sink, as if nudged
by a poltergeist, let it soak in its own juices. If only
you could escape noise, or at least turn it down a notch.

Second thoughts, why not immerse into babble,
make narrative from the symphony of the throng.
Even distant voices are charged by the exchange
of language and speech, each syllable given over
to meaning, to place, by the far reach of our minds.

Here, stories fall out of overheard fragments,
become different entities, sync, combine again.
You piece together more than your share of them
as they oscillate and transfer across to this space.
How sound can be re-embodied once dispossessed,
as it moves up and through these windows and walls.

THE PLASTER CAST FIGURES OF POMPEII

The method of taking plaster casts was introduced at Pompeii by Giuseppe Fiorelli, director of excavations between 1860 and 1875.

A glut of hydrocal pipelined to the heart
of an air gap – a body of air,
confined for two thousand years,

or perhaps not air at all
but what remains when cell-matter
is sealed, locked into the strata.

From a hairline crack
drawn across a bed of ash,
to a chiselled hollow, to this,

this moulded form, this human fossil,
remade, remodelled, real as flesh.
A cart driver, parodied by the absence

of a mule, is cast in his final act,
and might be praying in that fragmentary pose,
having let go of the trace, his hands

bound palm to palm and lifted up to his head,
his head bowed down to his hands.
Further along, a dog flips back

on itself as if upended or leaping
to catch a ball - hind legs playfully foetal,
open-mouthed to the possibility

of a last bark. A second human figure lies out
on a slab, appears to smile, like a groom
in the milliseconds before a post nuptial headshot.

THE MANY VERSIONS OF BRIAN ENO

Eno as a rare plumed bird
seen through a stained-glass window

Eno as a healing shaman reaching
into the psyche of the tuned-in

Eno as an androgynous poltergeist
moving through a wall of sound

Eno with his finger on the dial, flipping
the switch, mediating the gaps between

Eno as man on the road, lost soul, found soul,
searching for a niche, finding a niche

Eno joyfully shedding
all association with the niche

Eno as sampler of the dispossessed,
taste-maker, system chaser

Eno taking fortunes' direction
from the pack of letter-pressed cards

Eno sourcing the winter rain tapping his window,
mind-splicing it against a harp while laid-up

Eno catching the tail-end of the zeitgeist,
creating small moments that are big moments

Eno as man on the road, in a cabin
or in a stone studio commune in a forest

Eno snubbing morning walks
to go further into the synthesiser's void

Eno taking control of the ghost
in the machine, humanising its wail

REPLICA DUCKING STOOL

When we come to ask why they built this replica
and took it to the water's edge, will they say:
it provides a talking point, no harm done, *a bit of fun.*

No plaque here to remember the disembodied scolds
who, once tied in, were paraded to the city's artery,
raised aloft, mocked with gossip, then dropped.

There is no one to answer back on their behalf,
less still, to reset the recriminations, the sly injustices.
So much passes through here and leaves a residue.

Immersed in memes, updates, notifications,
tourists now gather by the bridge to idly chat.
Petrol and toxic foam form a question mark

on water weighted and baited by all it holds.
What floats to the top is merely half the story.
Still, voices find the surface, collect, then fall below.

I could give you names, stories, testimony,
but what good would it do here, or near here,
where nothing gives away a faithful account.

The river pulses with the unease and force of legacy,
saving its secrets so they can later be released,
without witnesses, at the filthy mouth of the estuary.

CO-SEISMIC SLIP

In the immediate after-shock,
He might have imagined the estate cracking
like a sheet of ice, cars shunting down
London Road bumper to bumper,
trees uprooted, telegraph poles upended,
scattered debris, split cables sparked
by the trailing legs of dazed cats and dogs.
He might have imagined that things
would be different in other ways too
but, really, what had changed in this room?

As the morning came to its usual standstill,
it was easy to think their lives would never move on
what with all this *stuff* stacked against the walls,
the curtains just about meeting, the goldfish
pulling faces at the aquatic screensaver,
the chair still turning its back, a record
left mid-song by a dust-clogged stylus,
a cold cup of coffee teetering on the brink.

And there she was lying next to him
as if nothing had happened, asleep of course.
The state he was in, who knows, perhaps
nothing had happened. Caffeine shakes,
residual work stress, all things mount up,
take their toll. What struck him though
was how change was a matter of perspective
and even that was temporal, remade at the edges.
Surely, what was called for was a decisive split,
yet, they were still here, in this small space,
playing it all out, fitting in all these parts.
Stone origins. Separation stage. Weathering away.

TENANCY DECANT

Now, Mrs O'Leary,
I know it's come as a shock
but you see the flat's not *yours*.
The Association owns it.

Let's just say you had it on extended loan
due to your predicament
and a whole list of *needs*
we assessed in your *Needs Assessment*.

Remember, when you needed us,
how you turned to us
with your three children
– each with their own complex *needs* –

and how we gladly placed you.
Look, the repairs
you desire are minor,
an inconvenience for sure, but minor,

and we've got to think of the public purse.
Naturally, there's a list

of people in situations
that are *worse*, much *worse*.

These people I talk of would die
for your level of support.
Believe me, if only you knew
how lucky you are

and we've another unit lined up.
Out of the area, yes; smaller, perhaps,
but suitable, appropriate –
I'd live there myself. We'll even help you

transfer your belongings,
just don't you worry.
We're very accommodating
to tenants that work

with us. Never you mind
what we'll do with it when you move.
We're your landlord, your *social* landlord.
We look after your interests.

Now tell me, when can I collect the keys?

DEDICATION TO CONNY PLANK

Home-spun, introvert-extrovert, stubborn, you
who gave Eno new ideas to take to Bowie
and how Bowie ran with them! Truth is you couldn't
care less about Bowie's next phase, not here
in your element, not in your own space and time.

Here, you are joyously-lost, oscillating, processing,
tape-looping, distorting the notes and non-notes
that suit. Here, you are stretching your giant-frame
across the wooden surface of the mixing desk.
With each arm you can reach any channel you wish.

In this studio you made from scratch and in the light
that spools and spools. Sound is absorbed into the walls
but doesn't leave the room. It only surges in intensity,
in its motorik momentum, building to something else
then something else again. Even your own son
is not allowed to know the code order of these sounds,
not yet at least. The code is your freedom for now.
He plays in the yard, oblivious. Your wife keeps it together
like a perfectly synthesized tune. Fine, if it's only melody
and harmony that you want. It's not.

What you seek, (I'm guessing), is a bold new sound
in this haunted state of '77, a getaway from glam,
a jump-lead for mainstream rock, a hippy rebellion,
communion with no need for countries or boundaries.
Like I say, I'm guessing, Conny, I'm reaching.
Am I on the right track?

THE VOICE

The voice that reads your finest work could almost be your own.
The way it holds each vowel and consonant, the way it softens
at vital moments, lilts, then shifts. This is more distinguished
than the low growling intonation you apply when well-oiled.

The voice is behind a screen behind a screen. Why no face?
Once you were the only source for *you*, or at least you thought so.
Now you're superseded by your upgrade; dare we say, *bettered*.
The voice's program has finessed its algorithm, advanced its code.

The voice adds gravitas, new words in places. Supplanted
by its dulcet tones, you search for your next creative *masterpiece*.
Even that could be pre-empted by the brain of the machine,
that scans and glides across the digital ether, plucking anapaests.

You were merely one input. Your impact on the scene was minimal.
Your ego is tracked and monitored even in sleep mode.
The analytics record you as a footnote in a minor publication,
credit you for turning-up in an age when turning-up was relevant.

GHOST STORY

Most people here know the story of the lady
that walks the wooded hill. On a cold winter's night,

a motorist, doing fifty, saw her step across the road.
Some details get missed out in the retelling

like the way she turned and looked straight through him.
He thought he'd hit her, *this lady* dressed in white,

and was so convinced he called the police.
But there was no one there when they came to search

and even they had heard the tale
of the mysterious shape that would walk across

back into the wood with no footprints or any other sign.
They told him not to overthink it.

This is what they recorded more than once:
a woman sees a moving car, steps in its way. No body found.

Sure, there was more behind the story
and how they placed her. Something about a husband

who had tormented her throughout their wedded life,
who, truly, was the reason for her sudden end and how,

in spite of him, she had a loving nature that never fell away.
She never even reported him for all he did.

Are there many other stories just like this? Hard to say.
They are widely told but the details are rarely traced.

THE GATECRASHERS

Old enough to know the way to oblivion and back
by Sunday lunch; young enough to think life
would always be like this. That night, spilled-out
into the car park for fresh air, we lay, face up,
on top of overblown flower beds, eyes to the sky,
our bodies imprinted in crushed stems.
In the old park pavilion – rented, mid-nineties,
for fifty quid – the DJ faded between each song.
Sometimes, by chance, they would match.
Blur or Oasis? Dance or indie rock?
We may never agree on that.
All the moving away, yet it's the same place
we return to. Those bricks and metal exit doors
embody what we fear is lost or going.
We fall into middle-years, no longer sure
as we were once in our teenage worlds.

Odd too, the way the party's gatecrashers –
lit by the strobe's roving eye – won't leave us.
Go outside, take another breath, and resummon how,
arriving late, lost to themselves, they stumbled in,
possessed by the spell of late adolescence.
Played over, they stumble still, just as we struggle
to move on through, reaching for a sign or handle.
We need to grip those things that help us
in the semidarkness as we go to another part
of that same space. Sober up, this time
we must hold on tighter. Just as back then,
the music swells inside our heads, as we try
to style-it-out, and make our way towards the light,
our better-selves still trying to keep in time.

THE FIZZOG TECHNIQUE
Inspired by Chris Cunningham's videos for Aphex Twin

Face it, Richard, we went face-to-face with you
because you had decided to invert your image,
to make it a totem, a dystopian vision

of opposition or just a mark of bare-faced cheek.
Face recognition, then blink, your visage
in a face-off between versions of you

pasted from the ponytailed stock-image,
transfigured into the dysmorphic distortions
more commonly found stretching the limits

of gesture and taste in a Hall of Mirrors.
We find you attached to a body not your own
but still moving in time to a riptide of glitches,

a chorus of *yous*. It is the lock-jaw grin
we can't shrug-off, that keeps us sleepless,
facing ourselves somehow, only to interrogate

a reflection, our reveal of eyes, mouth, bone;
that imprint we keep, or show, and think we own.

MEAT

Where the town backs onto wild-grass and wasteland,
sits spattered aggregate, orts of cloth and denim,
split bin bags of cast-offs tossed like jetsam.
The locals hope for a kill from the main spectacle.

As if on cue, two birds of prey circle overhead.
One breaks off, the other withdraws, gives way.
The parting of net curtains signals the sport
is about to begin. A family gathers, all eyes and wonder.

A man in his back-garden leans back, steadying his hips.
The decisive drop is first a blur from his binoculars,
but he refocuses the lenses when it grips. Captivated
by the live-action, he ignores his wife as she calls to him.

The bird departs, carving the sky; a small-partial-offering
is left, sickening, vibrant in its palette of pinks and reds.

CLUTTER JAR

...know that the distinction between past, present and future is only a stubbornly persistent illusion.
    — Albert Einstein

If it's true, and the future is as real as the past,
each new moment not so much
on the near brink of happening
as simply known from the point of view

of our knowing then why not lie here
on this bank of marram grass
and let the afternoon reveal a lukewarm reticence
to anything resembling honest light?

And all things being relative,
if our hungry eyes should fall on something
not quite expected – a money spider making its way
from blade to blade, the discovery

of a marble, its decorative coating chipped and cracked –
do not assume that the apparent passage
of movement, the longevity of contemplation,
is to be measured by seconds, minutes, hours,

nor that seeing can, in the grand scheme of things,
be put down to *now* – if *now* exists.
Find only sureness in our senses,
or in the sense of those things we store

in our mind's clutter-jar so we might recollect
what on earth it was that compelled us,
in a realm we called *the past*,
to not let go, to keep them there.

HABITAT ANALYSIS OF A CD AND RECORD FAIR

Shunned by those that search the cloud,
for us, the last of a tribe, this is the sweet spot.
No one disrespects the man at the door
who nods to a tune only found in his head.

We try not to show that we've noticed
his Pixies T-shirt is peppered with holes
and stained. A free-spirit, he looks nonplussed,
stamps our hands, goes back to nodding.

Inside, sounds compete for airspace:
drum & bass booms over Elvis,
blue-grass dominates electro-pop,
punk is overlaid by a burst of dub

that shakes the town hall, each timber of it,
as if it were an ear-drum. Traders lip-read prices
as middle-aged men riffle feverishly
through crates of tatty LPs. The smell

of BO ferments these taste-setters of their day
and the release of pheromone unites
in the same way they are united by the hunt
for the best theremin, hook or reverb.

A group of younger *Goth/ Emo/ Metal* sorts
are harder to categorise and are keen to explore.
They flex their leather trench-coats,
like discerning fruit-bats.

A speaker blows before the good bit.
We gather as one, punters and traders alike,
to gaze at the ruptured sub-woofer
as if it's an animal that's died.

In the *New Wave* section, a lad with a mohican,
still in his supermarket uniform,
holds a rare promo aloft, as if it were the answer
or a winning lottery ticket.

NEWLY ARRIVED

The neighbours each ask us why we left London.
What they really want to know is why we chose
to settle here of all places.

We have nothing much to tell them.
Given more time, we might mumble something
about commuting schedules, our passion

for the last red phone box. More romantically,
I might suggest I came here once, in an ecstatic daze,
a state of otherworldliness, then drifted to the edge

of the Great Stour and cupping my hands,
lent down to take the water. The neighbours
wouldn't buy it. No doubt, they've all conferred.

The house is still musty with the scent
of the previous owner, as if she never left.
Has she left? We never saw her leave.

Her mail still arrives with no forwarding address.
Marks and holes appear on the walls like scars.

The post-it notes that predate our time here
are highly cryptic, bordering on indecipherable.

On the second day, we dared each other
to go further into the storage spaces beneath
the stairs. The attic was left without a ladder.

On our third day, two giant buzzing beasts
urgently flew out through its hatch.
They buzzed mechanically, moved with precision,

seeming to carry some unknown inheritance,
or disinheritance, or existing between two entrances.
They did not appear again.

We are halfway through the fifth day now.
I really did see them, I say,
when you pull that face you pull.

BLUE PAINT

It sat there at the back of the shed
after being used once for an overcoat.
The lid slipped – for it had never been tightly
fixed. In truth, it dropped and fell through me.

It oozed into the cracks of the decked floor.
Thick, undiluted, sludge-like, it moved across
and onto my hands, as I tried to reverse
the direction of its flow back into the tub.

Despite my attempts to stop its spread,
it made its way into the house,
marked the sides and base of the sink,
sealed into the pores of my fingers, palms.

That's when I noticed you had it on you too,
as you crawled in from the garden
where you were playing with Buzzy Bee.
Subtle streaks signed off on each arm.

You cooed and babbled, oblivious
to the new bold highlight of *Blue Sky View*.
Not one of the toys had a fleck mark -
you were careful enough to protect them.

It would take an age to wash it off;
fading slowly, unapologetically.
Though you smiled, I winced, knowing
this arose from what I'd failed to grasp.

CIRCADIAN

A sudden upsurge, a dense murmuration
changing volume against a shapeshifting sky.
Is this an ending or the start of something?

The last bus takes you out to the coast.
You are lulled by its engine beneath your seat,
the intoxicating warmth and engine purr.

Hares beat their way up banks, burrow bound.
Trees tap and scrape the window glass.
The driver presses on, at speed, regardless

until the bus stops and the doors fling open.
Left by only a field, a track, you make your way.
Old rain seeps deep into your boots.

The outline of the guesthouse seems familiar,
as you finally approach. You feel the onrush
of heat as you enter and say your full name.

You'll wake to a single note of silence
that will fill up the room, as if intended to hold,
to pause everything in that one moment.

At which point, the world will break back in
with footsteps, early morning hushed voices,
the same flock resetting into their places again.

STARING AT BEASTS

From the vantage point of your highchair,
you are the first to spot the wood pigeon that patrols
our yard. It circles the perimeter, its bad leg healing
under the shabby protection of a patch of shade.

Because it is recuperating, immobile, we stare
up close. Its one-tone eye gives nothing away.
You giggle, I introduce the subject, you giggle more.
The routine goes like this. There is empathy here too.

We know what makes these beasts tick.
Take, Oscar, the bloated fish at the garden centre,
who was mouthing to you only last week.
His eyes boggled at the thought

we might only be passing through
his watching space. We knew he wanted us
to mime the meaning and shape of the life
beyond the tank, beyond even what he can see
of the reduced ceramic pots, cultivators, trowels.
We felt his sad glare at feeding time.

Your hands have grown inches this Spring alone.
Your face is longer than before, your first teeth
are coming through. Every change leaves me
like that fish. Everything I think I know
is challenged beautifully and made again.
I am learning all your mannerisms.
This world keeps spinning its tale,
never quite stopping the clock.

STORY OF THE WHEELTAPPER'S SON

No one knows these days
what a tapper even was.
Go on, ask them on the platform,
see what they say. That dopey lot,
standing there, calling themselves
rail staff, when all they do is stretch
and yawn and wait out their time.
From the thirties, my father was one,
a proud unionised tapper that is.
He'd tap the train wheel with a hammer
at specific points and he'd listen
in real close and with care
like a concert conductor does.
What mattered was the exact type
of sound it made and for how long.
If it came at the optimum decibel
with its metal frame ringing true
that made it right and proper.
He'd tick off a sheet as he moved down
the track. He was stern and upright,
You wouldn't want to cross him.
He'd seen out several campaigns
before the tapping, the settling down,
but never spoke on it, you didn't then.
I can still see him as he was.
He's shouting something to me
in his work clothes before setting off.
I can just about make out the sound
of his boots crunching gravel
in the yard, the locking of the gate.

That stinging feeling on my spine
from where he'd used a belt.
It's all still with me, it's all so clear.
He's making his way down again.

REMOTE

Before they made him totally remote,
he travelled routinely to this glass box every day.
He is taking pictures of it for the last time
before moving on to the next *opportunity*.
The latest glass box has lost its glint.
In truth, he's hardly been here for years
meaning that nostalgia has no place
in his mind – now shrinking, as it swims
in its own juices towards retirement age –
and he's piecing together the shards
of what it was: breakout-area posturing,
canteen food ratings, a surfeit of water coolers.
But something gets him – not just this workplace
but all his former workplaces which he knows
are emptied out. These unpeopled shells define him.
He's taken a picture of all the places he ever worked in.
All those hours travelling to glass boxes
and now nothing, no destination. Were they worth it?
All those albums he listened to, on loop,
or just the slow repeat of his own breath.
What did this all mean? Others looked at him too
whilst weighing-up the same dilemmas
and occupying his air space on a variety
of overly burdened commuter trains.
He would glare back not registering a thing.
Every carriage back then was occupied
by those phasing out and into the space behind
their own glazed eyeballs. Deep down
in his unconscious, unhooked from the trained part
of his brain, came a reoccurring image
of slowly sloshing water, of fires going out.

REWIND, PLAY, PAUSE

Back when we still played cassettes and shared them
with an emboldened cover-doodle,
a list of songs taken from late-night radio, cribbed notes

on an underground scene to pass on and later deny existed;
when we encountered itchy earphone foam
on the last bus home, watching the wonder of its small form

in our hot hands and the matching to rollers, idlers, capstans,
all turning over like a flax wheel
until the tape wore to a base layer of polyester-film,

and you could hear a dull reeling just under the music
but, regardless, you kept on going,
until the winding down of it all and the very last click.

*

Back when you spoke to the same cashier -
when there was a cashier –
and *the till* was a place to be advised by this person

who knew what you needed even though you didn't
and you thought nothing of it
until they were gone and replaced by a scanner

meaning that some days you now speak to no one at all,
returning only to face a window that looks across
to a church high-up on the hill, a heroic line of trees

and a fresh-coat of sky, occasionally so clear, so beautiful,
that the feeling of joy in your chest
can be held onto when the next day comes with a new tone.

*

Back when the ticket inspector's steady accumulation
of quips were the journey's sole measure,
gradually instilling a sense of place inside your gut

that, at the time, you never really placed a value on
and which now you'd openly miss,
if *missing* was accepted currency for this kind of loss.

*

Back when what we earnt was not packaged
then gambled by spinners,
sometimes against a whim or theory so baseless,

when played to the end of a cryptic value chain,
even ivory towers might shatter
from the force of the resulting hurricane.

*

Back when your health was not a search or app
with a diagnostic plan that tells you when to sleep,
how far to walk, the likely year of your *unfortunate* death,

which reminds you that all you really require is that doctor
who told you, once, he understood and meant it,
and seemed to make time in a surgery that's now closing.

*

Back when our actions lent our voices familial notes,
not requiring voice recognition into a tablet,
and our lives weren't mapped by a sequence of code

that reduced us to raw data that predicted yet more data;
when each day was not prescribed before conception
so that we could believe we were making our own recording.

NIGHT TIME PRAM PUSHERS' CLUB

We - who were born unknowing, the sleepy-headed
of our species, who are clumsy in this field of rearing
with always much to learn after the first learning.

We - who walk the streets of the village in the dark –
yes, always in the dark – with prams held out
like mechanical appendages to our unfit frames.

We - who watch the horizon with hope
of seeing the last vestiges of nautical twilight,
yet experience only sore necks from that searching.

We - who ride rough-shod over kerbs,
passing public houses with a sense
of the forlorn.

We - who when we see each other nod, say
alright, mate, as if we are pushing
dodgems at a fairground.

We - who see in each other's eyes,
some kind of recognition in the shared
experience of our designated duty.

We - who have lost more dummies – whilst lulled
to a dream-state by iPad download lullabies –
than we care to mention.

We - who are too scared to talk to other pram pushers
because to do so would break some arcane code
that preserves peace in the hour where all is silent.

We - who find ourselves surprised
to find the last stop is a front door – a home.
Inside, is a whole life playing out before us.

We – who are just as surprised to discover
we are yet to wake up, that our little passengers
were the ones who navigated each crossing and turn.

ACKNOWLEDGEMENTS

'Before the Clinking of Glasses' first appeared in *Dream Catcher*.

'Experts' – previously titled 'Prospective Density of Snow' – was shortlisted in the Canterbury Poet of the Year Competition (2023).

'The Old Crowd' was Highly Commended in the Walter Swan Poetry Prize (Ilkley Literature Festival).

'Shaoshan' first appeared in *The Verve Anthology of Protest* (Selected and Introduced by Kim Moore) and was Commended in the Verve Poetry Competition 2023 on the theme of 'Protest'.

'Posthumous' first appeared in *SOUTH*.

'Something Not Quite Placed' appeared in *Poetry London*.

'Plastic Seahorses' was commended in the Ware Poets Open Poetry Competition 2023.

'The Plaster Cast Figures of Pompeii' first appeared with *Ink, Sweat and Tears*.

'Replica Ducking Stool' first appeared in *Acumen*.

'Co-Seismic Slip', 'Ghost Story' and 'Night Time Pram Pushers' Club' first appeared in *New Welsh Review*.

'The Gatecrashers' is shortlisted in the Ver Poets Open Competition 2025 and will appear in the competition anthology

'Meat' first appeared in *Magma*.

'Fizzog Technique' first appeared in *You've got so many machines, Richard! An anthology of Aphex Twin poetry (Broken Sleep Books)*.

'Clutter Jar' first appeared in *The North*.

'Habitat Analysis of a CD and Record Fair' appeared in *Masculinity: An Anthology of Modern Voices (Broken Sleep Books, 2024)*.

'Newly Arrived' first appeared with *The London Magazine*.

'Blue Paint' appeared in *Masculinity: An Anthology of Modern Voices (Broken Sleep Books, 2024)*.

'Staring at Beasts' was commended in the Ware Poets Open Poetry Competition 2023.

LAY OUT YOUR UNREST

www.ingramcontent.com/pod-product-compliance
Lightning Source LLC
LaVergne TN
LVHW041326080426
835513LV00008B/614